ONCE THERE WAS A TREE

Books by Phyllis S. Busch and Arline Strong

ONCE THERE WAS A TREE
   The Story of the Tree, A Changing Home for Plants and Animals

LIONS IN THE GRASS
   The Story of the Dandelion, A Green Plant

Once There Was a Tree

THE STORY OF THE TREE, A CHANGING HOME
FOR PLANTS AND ANIMALS

by Phyllis S. Busch

Photographs by Arline Strong

THE WORLD PUBLISHING COMPANY

CLEVELAND AND NEW YORK

All the photographs in this book are by Arline Strong with the exception of the following, which are reproduced here by courtesy of the National Audubon Society: on page 16, by Henry M. Mayer; on page 25, by Hugh M. Halliday; on page 26, by Karl H. Maslowski; on page 27, by Robert C. Hermes; on page 28 and on the back of the jacket, by Allan D. Cruickshank; on pages 29, 30, and 33, by Leonard Lee Rue III; on page 34, by Arthur W. Ambler; on page 38, by Alvin E. Staffan; on page 39, by Stuart M. Smith. The publishers gratefully acknowledge permission to reproduce these photographs.

Published by The World Publishing Company
2231 West 110th Street, Cleveland, Ohio 44102
Published simultaneously in Canada by
Nelson, Foster & Scott Ltd.
Library of Congress catalog card number: 68-14685
Text copyright © 1968 by Phyllis S. Busch
Illustrations copyright © 1968 by Arline Strong
All rights reserved. No part of this book may be reproduced
in any form without written permission from the publisher, except for
brief passages included in a review appearing in a newspaper
or magazine. Printed in the United States of America.
Designed by Jack Jaget.

FOR BEN

AUTHOR'S FOREWORD

This book is planned to encourage the very young child to experience his environment esthetically as well as intellectually— with his heart as well as his mind.

The approach used is designed to stimulate children to learn by inquiry rather than by mere passive acceptance of stated facts. Thus the child is led to explore and to discover for himself the wonders and beauty of the world of nature.

A perfect first introduction to the study of ecology, this picture book tells the fascinating story of how a living tree becomes a log, and how it and its accompanying varieties of plants and animals interact with each other and with their environment.

No matter how lonely a tree looks, it is never alone.
A tree has company all the time.

You will always find birds,
insects, and other animals,
as well as plants,
living in it, on it, under it,
and around it.

Some birds' nests swing high in the branches of a growing tree.
You might notice the bird cradle of an oriole hanging in the treetops.
The mother may be off looking for food for her little ones.

Perhaps you see what looks like a big
untidy basketball made of leaves.
This was a gray squirrel's summer house.

Among the lower branches of a tree
you might spot the nest
of a wood thrush.
This bird's song fills the woods
with beautiful music.
The wood thrush,
like many other birds,
feeds on some of the insects
which damage trees
by eating their leaves.
One such insect
is the tent caterpillar.
You can find their filmy tents
all over the bushes and trees
in the springtime.

Down in the lower leaves of a tree you might see tiny green insects,
called aphids, which suck plant juices from the leaves.
On the trunk of a tree you will probably see unusual
kinds of plants growing, called lichens, which cover the bark.
These lichens—gold, green, gray, and yellow—look especially plump
and pretty after a rain.

And, if you look at the foot of a tree in the early spring, you may find a tiny, colorful flower show.

Some of the things that live in a tree
are helpful to the tree, like the wood thrush,
but other things can harm the tree.
Sometimes tiny beetles make small holes in the tree
and dig tunnels under the bark as they look for food
and a place to lay their eggs.
In order to live and to grow, a tree
must get food to all its parts.
Too many holes and tunnels will cut
the tree's food supply and the tree will starve.

For the same reason, a tree will starve if a person tears off a piece of bark
all around the tree trunk. The tree cannot get food to its lower parts and so it dies.
Or, there may not be enough birds to eat the caterpillars which feed upon the tree's leaves.
The tree, like all other green plants, uses its leaves to make its food.
If too many leaves are eaten by caterpillars, the tree will not be able to make the food
it needs in order to live and so it will starve.

Other things can happen to a tree to weaken it.
Sometimes a tree will become infected with spores from fungus plants.
Spores are tiny specks so small that you can barely see them.
They fall into a crack in the tree where they grow into fungus plants
which look like tangled pieces of white thread. If you look under the bark
of a tree, you may find some of these fungus threads growing there.

Later, on the outside of a tree—on the trunk—some fungus plants form what looks
like a row of shelves. These shelves are the parts of the fungus plant
where new spores are grown. As the wind blows, it lifts up the ripe spores
formed inside the shelves and carries them off to other trees.
If there are too many fungus plants on one tree,
the tree will become soft and weak, and finally it will die.

Or a branch might be broken
off a tree, leaving a hole
in its place.
Rain water collects in the hole.
The wood around it becomes soft
and decays. Insects enter the hole
and begin chewing away at the wood,
making more holes. Fungus spores
fall in and start to grow.

If you see a tree that has many fungus plants or holes in it, you can be fairly sure that it is dead, even though it is still standing up.

All sorts of insects live in a dead tree.
Wood-boring beetles make small holes in the bark.
Carpenter ants tunnel through the wood, looking for the beetles.
As the dead tree begins to decay, it becomes soft and grows weaker.
Now other kinds of living things are attracted to it.
Each one of them will make or use a hole of a different size.

A downy woodpecker flies by and finds
a hole where it will build a nest.

Hairy woodpeckers chip away
at the tree as they search
for ants or make a hole
in which to nest.

A large hole left
by a falling branch
might be used by
a flying squirrel.
These animals leap
through the air
from tree to tree
but they are seldom seen
because they do
their leaping at night.

If there is another hole about
the same size as the flying squirrel's,
a screech owl might move in.

Sometimes a hole in a dead tree
is large enough for
an entire family of raccoons . . .

. . . or even a bear, looking for a place to spend part of the winter.

The holes increase in size
and number until there are more
holes than tree and the dead tree
becomes too weak to stand.
A storm . . . or a strong wind . . .
and the tree topples over.

The fallen tree is a log.

Many different kinds of living things are drawn to a log just as they were to a tree.

Where the tree's roots were in the ground there is now a pit.
A fox may choose to make his den here.

The hollow trunk might become
a skunk's home.

Soon it begins to rain, wetting the log and the earth around it.
Snakes, salamanders, frogs, and toads move in underneath the log where it is cool and moist.

The rain softens the log
and it begins to rot.
Under the rotting bark
is a good place to look
for little gray sow bugs.
Here you might also find
centipedes and slugs.

In the winter the log can barely be seen as it lies under a blanket of snow.

But animal tracks in the snow
show that the log still has company.
The mice, rabbits, and squirrels
which seek its protection
know it is there.

Warmer weather melts the snow, turning it to water.
Mosses of different kinds grow in soft, fuzzy patches on the moist log.
Lichens cover what is left of the bark. Ferns begin to grow there too.
The log now looks like a little garden.

The inside of the log gets softer all the time.
Reach into it and take a handful of tree.
It is now soft and crumbly and brown.

Spring brings more rain.
The moisture and warmth make the log decay more quickly.

The log is becoming
part of the soil.
It loses the shape of a tree.
Whatever nourishment is left
in the log enriches
the earth around it.

A tree seed might land on this rich, moist soil and begin to grow.

Then the life of a tree will start once more.

Perhaps one day you will be taking a walk with your grandchildren
and come again to the spot where the old log used to be.
And you can tell them the story of how once there was another tree
in that place and how it had a beginning, and an end, and company all the time.

ABOUT THE AUTHOR

PHYLLIS BUSCH, who is a science teacher, received her training at Hunter College, New York University, and Cornell University. The author of many publications on science and conservation, she has taught at every level—elementary school, junior high school, high school, college, and graduate school. Dr. Busch is now Executive Director of New York State's federal project SPRUCE (Science Project Related to Upgrading Conservation Education). She and her husband live in Stanfordville, New York.

ABOUT THE PHOTOGRAPHER

ARLINE STRONG is a skilled photographer who has illustrated many handsome science and nature books with her beautiful photographs. Her pictures have appeared in a number of exhibits and displays, including a one-woman show at New York's American Museum of Natural History. Originally a fashion photographer, she became interested in photographing nature as a result of her two sons' fascination with the world of science. She and her family live in Riverdale, New York.

1   2   3   4   5   72   71   70   69   68